makar/unmakar

MAKAR/ UNMAKAR

twelve contemporary poets in scotland

juana adcock / tessa berring
callie gardner / harry josephine giles
colin herd / daisy lafarge
nicky melville / iain morrison
nat raha / maria sledmere
alice tarbuck / kate tough

edited by calum rodger

Published in 2019 by **Tapsalteerie** | 9 Anderson Terrace, Tarland, Aberdeenshire, AB34 4YH | www.tapsalteerie.co.uk | ISBN: 978-1-9162148-0-4 | Copyright remains with the respective poets | 'The Serpent Dialogue' by **Juana Adcock** was published in Spanish in *Kokoro*, and English in *Split* (Blue Diode Press, 2019) | **Tessa Berring**'s 'Shock' was published in *Rialto Poetry*, issue 89, 'Playing House' in *Datableedzine*, issue 10, 'Embrace Me' in *Adjacent Pineapple*, issue 1, 'Real Sea' in *South Bank Poetry*, issue 10 | **Callie Gardner**'s poems 'springletter' and 'summerletter' previously appeared in *naturally it is not* (The 87 Press, 2018); 'all my tentacles' previously appeared in *Chicago Review* 62; 1-3, winter 2018-19 | Versions of **Harry Josephine Giles**'s poems have been published in *Orkney Stoor* (Abersee Press, 2015) and *Multiverse* (Shoreline of Infinity, 2018) | **Colin Herd** would like to acknowledge *Unfettering Poetry: The Fancy in British Romanticism*, by Jeffrey Robinson, from where he found the concept of 'fanciphobia' | Some of **Daisy Lafarge**'s poems first appeared in *understudies for air* (Sad Press, 2017), *Poetry Review*, summer 2017, and *The Scotsman*, January 2018. 'Capriccio' was published by SPAM Press in 2019 and a selection was published in *The Stinging Fly*, summer 2019 | **nicky melville**'s poem 'an expression of natural language' was published in *Otoliths* and 'corpoem one' in *The Projectionist's Playground* | **Iain Morrison**'s 'The Huff, the Stand-off, the Counter-huff' was published in *Along Huff Lane* (Moschatel Press, 2016), and 'Don'cha Don'cha' was published in *I'm a Pretty Circler* (Vagabond Voices, 2018) | **Nat Raha**'s 'sonnet ("joy graze the tones of you")' was published in *countersonnets* (Contraband Books, 2013). 'untitled ("our intensive support")' and 'untitled ("here in the diaspora")' were published in *of sirens, body & faultlines* (Boiler House Press, 2018) | 'Object Sheltering' by **Maria Sledmere** appeared in issue two of *CUMULUS* | **Kate Tough**'s 'Caitlin' and 'Islip' previously appeared in *tilt-shift* (Tapsalteerie, 2016).

INTRODUCTION:
CALUM RODGER

Makar/Unmakar: Twelve Contemporary Poets in Scotland presents generous selections from a dozen of the finest and most vital poets writing outside the mainstream in Scotland today. It makes no claims to geographical, generational or stylistic comprehensiveness, and far less to some spurious notion of 'Scottishness'. But while there is much more to individuate these poets than to group them (even a cursory glance through these pages reveals an extraordinary range of formal, linguistic, psychological and affective approaches), their poetics are united by a common attitude, which might best be defined as a refusal of complacency. In other words, a recognition that there are no givens in language, as there are no givens in life, and that the craft of poetry entails what Veronica Forrest-Thomson called, in a different context, 'dismantling': a taking apart in order to put back together, not merely for its own sake, but – insofar as language is the means by which we make sense of the world – to challenge and offer alternatives to our 'given' conceptions of the world, and our place within it. Or to be, as this anthology would have it, unmakar and makar.

Because 'makar' – the old Scots word for poet – is a rich and complex word, and one that has made something of a comeback in recent years. Traditionally applied to the royal court poets of the fifteenth and sixteenth centuries, the Scottish Government's instatement of the Scots Makar in 2004 (a post held to date by

Edwin Morgan, Liz Lochhead, and currently Jackie Kay) has once again woven this word into the fabric of Scottish civic and cultural life. Most Scottish cities now boast their own Makars and increasing numbers of towns and regions are following suit. These are Makars-with-a-capital-M who, like their courtly forebears, participate in public discourse from a position of governmental patronage or sponsorship. That contemporary Scotland supports such a role for poetry is a fact worth celebrating, but as with all our democratic institutions it should not be celebrated uncritically. This critical spirit is there in Morgan, Lochhead and Kay, to their great credit. But the danger remains that this sense of 'Makar' reduces the word to mere mantle – a civic appellation – and thus risks occluding some of its richest meanings, its complexity, and perhaps (what would be even worse) the kind of poetry that thrives beyond such narrow limits – not least the poetry in the present anthology. If this word is to mean anything beyond a state-sponsored epithet, it too must be dismantled.

This leads us back to the etymological root of the word: from the Ancient Greek *poiesis*, poet as maker. According to this emphasis, the poet's concern here is less with the civic than with the formal, perhaps even the ontological: the more-or-less conscious play and struggle with the craft of language, with the challenges of making something *mean* (or, more radically, *be*) for oneself and others. Of recent history, three poets stand out in this regard: Forrest-Thomson, WS Graham and Ian Hamilton Finlay. Whether in Forrest-Thomson's 'artifice' or Graham's 'constructed space', here are formalist foils to the discursive emphases of Morgan, Lochhead and Kay. But we should be wary of drawing too strict an opposition between these poles of poetic practice (and not just because 'dueling polarities' is an overused trope in Scottish literary criticism). A decisive precursor here is Tom Leonard, in whose work poetic form and civic responsibility are inseparable. As 'all livin language is sacred', so the drive to make and unmake both living and language are, in the last analysis, one and the same.

So too for the poets in *Makar/Unmakar*. Each approaches the 'being' of the poem with a degree of consciousness and conscience in lineage with fellow dismantlers Forrest-Thomson, Graham and Hamilton Finlay. Yet their work follows too from the gains made (and confirmed, nominally at least, by the officiality of Makardom) by Morgan, Lochhead and Kay, who overcame the stiflingly masculinist and heteronormative homogeny of twentieth century Scottish poetry through chameleonic experimentation, omnivorous internationalism, and boldly revitalised approaches to performance and the presentation of identity. As in Leonard's work, the poets' refusal of complacency in this anthology is at once formal *and* social, and inseparably so. To quote Leonard again, it is a poetry 'responsible to that world / – and responsible for that world', with 'that world' both the formal world(s) constituted by the poem itself, and the social and physical world(s) which the poem, its makar and its readers inhabit.

As such, 'makar' is best understood – as the wealth of definitions given in the *Dictionary of the Older Scottish Tongue* demonstrate – not as polar, but spectral. It encompasses not just the literary ('author'; 'poet'), but the crafted in all its guises ('one who fashions, constructs, produces, prepares'), along with the metaphysical ('God'), the ecological ('Nature'), the performative ('one who performs some action'), the legislative ('one who promulgates a law'), and even the militaristic ('one who appoints knights'). It is an invaluable word, not because it presents a shortcut to a lazy and banal source of national pride, but because its richness and complexity suggest something more basic and universal, perhaps even essential: the multifaceted, world-making dimensions poetic language can take, at every level of human experience and endeavour. You'll find every one of these definitions in various colours and compounds in poems of this anthology. Indeed, the vitality and value of this poetry consists in rendering the whole spectrum visible, audible – which is to say *felt*, and thinkable.

Such is the thinking behind the title of this anthology: makar/ unmakar; making and unmaking poetry and life in all its spectra. And unlike makars of the previous century such as Graham and Finlay, both of whom lived in a kind of peripatetic exile, these poets (though they come from all corners of Scotland and in some cases further afield) have made their homes in the metropolitan centres of Edinburgh and Glasgow. Each, in their distinctive ways, make of poetry a shared enterprise, through such multifarious activities as collaboration, translation, zine and small press publishing, workshops, events, research, criticism, and pedagogy. They are also very fine performers, and opportunities to experience their poetry live should not be missed. Perhaps these priorities are in part a consequence of the 'given' world they are presented with – one of austerity and precarity, reactionary right-wing populism (aka fascism), violently retrogressive attitudes to gender and sexuality, surveillance capitalism and ecological catastrophe. This is not to say all the work in this anthology is 'political' poetry, narrowly defined. Invariably, however, it is poetry concerned with the relationships between making and being, between language and living, and how such making and unmaking occurs not in isolation, but necessarily in the building of connections, communities, consensus – shared frameworks for making meaning, and a cohabitable place in the world.

A word, finally, on the decision to include twelve poets in the anthology; it would not, after all, have been difficult to fill an anthology twice or three times this size. The primary reason was logistic, so that each poet's work has space to breathe and develop (especially in respect of Tapsalteerie's primary identity as a pamphlet press). But an additional appeal came from another anthology almost fifty years old: *Twelve Modern Scottish Poets*, designed as a textbook for high school students and edited by

Charles King. Its rollcall comprises an all-male cast of the doyens of the Scottish Renaissance, its only real outlier Morgan, both for his cosmopolitan idiom and his (then closeted) sexuality. In this respect (and, it is hoped, many others) the present anthology could not be more different. That said, while a number of recent anthologies have made valuable contributions to the process, at once arduous and rapturous, of redressing the representational imbalance which has long beleaguered poetry in Scotland, *Makar/Unmakar* was never explicitly conceived in these terms. Rather, it's simply the case that much of the best poetry in Scotland today is being written by voices hitherto suppressed by the established hierarchies of the poetry world. Nor should this be in any way surprising; the only surprise is that such voices, to our great detriment, have been suppressed and neglected for so long. This is not to pitch the present anthology as a riposte to King's. But it hopefully helps to assert, at the very least, that previous generations' failure to acknowledge, to read and to celebrate a great deal of great poetry need not be our own. It suggests, moreover, that these poets' refusal of complacency is no stylistic fancy, but a fundamental ontological imperative.

It remains only to thank the poets for accepting the invitation to contribute to the anthology, and for their generosity in sharing their work and at every stage of the editorial process; they have made my work as editor a pleasure. Thank you also to Katy Hastie and Henry Bell for their indispensable feedback and advice. While this introduction has painted with the broadest of brushstrokes, each poet's selection is prefaced with a brief note designed to illuminate the poems and to point the reader towards more of their work. Seek them out, in print, online, and in performance. As their work unequivocally and polyphonically demonstrates, it is a rare time to read a makar in Scotland. Long may it continue, and in the meantime, may you make and unmake of these poems everything you will.

JUANA ADCOCK

For Juana Adcock poetry is what gets found in translation. Her work thrives at the porous borders between lands, lives and languages, with her first collection *Manca* (Tierra Adentro, 2014) written largely in Spanish but featuring several poems in which Spanish and English tongues clash and blend both within and between lines. It's a dizzying and delightful experience to read, even more so to hear in performance, and it's this attentiveness to translation in all its forms – as mediation between self and other, body and world – that makes her poetry so vital in our technologically-mediated present. In one poem from *Manca*, for example, a fallen microphone 'breaking off / the accent key' leads the speaker to conclude 'Thou shalt renounce your own language'. Similar concerns underpin the present selection, taken from Adcock's collection *Split* (Blue Diode Press), whose notes of curiosity, anguish and longing are laced with a subversive, serpentine venom.

The Serpent Dialogues

(an extract)

5

But the snake also had violent mood swings, and the woman suffered immensely for it. Some days he gave her the most fascinating answers, other days he was silent, or sarcastic.[1] That's when the woman started to doubt her own sanity, wondering whether she was the one who was in his space,[2] the balcony not being hers but his, with him being gracious enough to allow her to visit. But even when the snake was in the foulest mood, the woman never wanted to sever the connection, because she felt their dialogues always taught her something. In this respect, the woman was a formalist.[3]

1. Let go, foot of snow
   melt in hand, melt in sun

2. A fundamental error of attribution
   eggs most fiction on:
   to say "mine", "his", "hers"
   to call ourselves the owners
   as we walk through the forest
   along trails built by the tread of wolves

3. O heartbreak, old friend!
   We preferred to live off the fault lines,
   where the pressure builds and rock is lifted.
   In the shoogling of things
   in our hermit huts
   in a place of tension
   never resting!
   I wanted to tell you how much
   our conversations shook up my mind,
   set me forth
   into a movement of planets.
   But already I could feel you touch the valley of my neck
   and wrap your fingers around.
   As you gently squeezed, I could see you flirt
   with the idea of strangulation.
   Already feeling the glottis
   close in your grip
   I implored, "Let's live together in a tiny room
   and drive each other crazy. It's what lovers
   do!

6

w: Snake, what's the true nature of desire?

s: Everyone asks me that. Don't you have anything more interesting to talk about? That's like asking the moon about the mysteries of love

w: OK, what's your opinion on Rumi's poem about the mouse and the frog?

s: Is that something like the little mermaid? I can't stand stories about princesses

w: Human induced climate change and mass extinction of the species. You must have strong opinions on that

s: Terrible. What else?

w: What do you do when you can't sleep?

s: I don't sleep. What else?

Then one day the snake didn't show up at all. Her mind scrambled for an explanation for what had happened, whether she'd said or done something offensive, whether she'd misunderstood. She called out from her balcony all day long: Snake! Snake!

It occurred to her it might be some sort of demonstration on his part, a lesson on the structure of desire itself. She cut out a rectangle in the middle of a blank page. She gazed into that window: *look at where desire lives*, she told herself. She made lists of things the snake might be trying to teach her about desire:

1. to create desire you must play with expectation: create a pattern, then break it
2. desire is a friendly embrace that suddenly turns electric
3. desire draws a rosette that starts at the chest and then dances around the whole body
4. desire is also the impulse to run away from what we've done

She thought absence was the snake's method, and she paid attention like a loyal disciple. She began waiting at the balcony two hours earlier than the usual time, observing desire as it swerved around inside her flesh: a rabid monkey thrashing against metal bars. She took note of the shapes, colours, tastes of its rage. She kept a journal, to analyze all its components:

Day 19

The sky continues to grumble like a hungry belly.

Day 21

The phone vibrates and I obey
rising from my chair where I am nestled with a book
I listen as the sun
draws a rib bone across the sky

I remember an artist who operated on himself
cut open his own chest,
carved out a rib bone,
sewed himself back up,
offered the bone to his mother
as a necklace,
and she, half guiltily, half glad,
obliged. What art
can ever be made after this?

Day 22

To befriend my boredom, my wanting.
To notice how it takes hold of me.
How, when I decided otherwise,
and went on a long walk
wearing sandals, despite threats of rain,
I paid attention to this pulse, to the way
the plants shook
and quivered in the wind, as if in perpetual
longing. This longing
also a part
of –

And then
words, mixing lust and tenerezza,
appear unexpected on my screen.

The sky roars, annoyed
at my distractedness.

It seems all I care about is
this impossible encounter, an instant
through the bits and bytes,
up to the stratosphere, through a satellite
then back to earth again:

✓✓ *seen 22:03*

Am I really –

All we've
ever
really
wanted
is
to be seen.

To be scene:
watched, contemplated
accepted

Day 23

In the big room, in the church, the place I was so afraid of at night.
I finally come here to work.
To be without internet, to get right down to it.

And I discover the mirror I have been without all these days.
The mirror I never wanted to see myself in. That in the dark I was
     so afraid of.

Switching on the light, those two seconds of terror before the
     tungsten blinks.
The terrible silence of knick knacks, flung
the broken musical instruments
their tune like the skeleton
of a mouse in formol

And I watch as
my brain turns to my phone: wanting wanting wanting

Day 24

In my body, full of scrolling. Scrolls of the dead sea, always down, down, not reaching. Always eating but never nourished. Mistaking this hunger for a particular need, rather than a dis-ease. Before television, we used to sit round the fire and perform for each other. We still do, but in a way that makes us feel utterly alone. Our faces lit by the blue light of the fire-screen.

I Google this, and the internet says that what I'm feeling is completely normal, that there are hundreds of thousands of people like me, scattered around the globe. We tell each other our most dreadful secrets, this is our way to be home. My fingers like crabs, moving sideways on the keyboard. I wanted always to be by your side. It didn't matter to me that you were a miser, dry kindling, half of your body crushed by heartbreak, and that you no longer believed in life. I wanted to hook onto your arm and walk through the streets, heels clapping against cobblestone, and feel protected.

To instead be one's own wife –

Day 25

I post a selfie

take myself sweetly

to the stage
or the altar

bring myself flowers
and rain

Day 26

I reach for my phone
to check the time
when I can't remember the word
to be entertained
when something hurts, to see what it means
when I can't remember the way
when I know the way but want to make sure
when I don't know the train times
when I know the train times but want to make sure
when the sun is setting, igniting a bridge in the sky
to document this moment
to experience this moment
to experience myself documenting this moment
to document myself experiencing myself documenting
        a moment I'm experiencing
when I'm lonely, to see what others are doing

when I'm uninformed, to see what others are broadcasting
when I can't remember the lyrics, or the tune, to this song
to do my shopping, while at the gym
to open my yoga app, while at work
to arrange a date, while on the toilet
to read an article, while walking from A to B
to check my email, while in the queue at the post office
to see, just to see, if anyone remembered me today
to be annoyed, if someone insists on an earlier message
    I forgot to respond to

my phone to fill in all the gaps

Day 27

To paraphrase the cheesy Charlie Chaplin meme
I saw in a picture frame on the pizzeria wall today:
silence is gold; we tend to buy noise instead.

And something about reaching for my phone as a form of
noise or interference, like wanting
to be saved from experiencing this instant
with all its beautiful and devastating aloneness

Day 28

The internet tells me that
Hiraeth is Welsh for
"homesickness for a home that you cannot
return to, or that never was"

I am split between this word and its exact opposite:
"a feeling of being at home in the unknown
in which you always are,
and which has always been"

TESSA BERRING

Reading Tessa Berring's poetry is a curious and often disquieting experience, like encountering a pinned butterfly in a museum and fancying you just saw its wings beat. Berring works extensively in collaboration and translation, with her pamphlet *Cut Glass and No Flowers* (Dancing Girl Press, 2016) followed by her first full collection *Bitten Hair* (Blue Diode Press, 2019). There is an intimacy and charm to her poems which belies, as Berring herself puts it, 'something repressed/uncomfortable around the edges'; poems in which (to quote e.e. cummings) 'feeling is first', made palpable in a tense and tentative construction of form and surprise. While that feeling is irrepressibly human, her work can also approach an almost object-like solidity, as if 18th century automata have developed agency and are performing various states of being in a twilit workshop of 'lean words [...] and lightly placed / unspeakable things'.

Playing House

I'd like a golden apple, or a red one
or I'll cry

(this room is so tiny
when covered in snow)

did you hear about the woman

who bound her face
in hot spun sugar

as a protest against everything?

we could do things too
like breathing in, then out

oh my God, oh my God
you'd really love that, wouldn't you!

Embrace Me

Skin is wipe clean
and my jeans fit well

and once I wrote about
my dream with men in it

all cotton wool heads!

I chopped them off
of course

which was bloody
like tampons

and my hands stank
of dead petunia

it was a good story
nuanced and delicate

someone said

though they might not
have meant it

it's a relief about skin
being easy to wipe

and it's good having jeans
all over my legs

I like lean words
you know, like spirit

and lightly placed
unspeakable things

Apple Core

When he fucks her
she feels

like an apple core

an apple core
or a snail

knotted in it's shell

at least, this is how
it used to be

until she discovered

that tickling the back
of the air

with her cold pink toes
was funny

she can pretend to
be wearing stilts

but upside down

Shock

The floor is drenched in green disinfectant
the monkey is limp, blue, decapitated

come and examine my grid!

I use it to mark gradations of red
from pink through blush to scarlet

it is utterly harmless
like listening to string partitas is harmless

when you no longer talk to your pet

I used to talk to cats *(miaow, miaow, miaow)*
but not any more

I greet them in silence as if they are furred spectres
with no language I can share – idiot!

the monkey is limp – did I mention that?

or that all I ask for is an expression of grace
and that you come to me when I

am recumbent and comfortable
my electric friend

before colour fades, as it always fades

amaranth, sunset, peppercorn,
raspberry, hellebore, blood

If Things Stay Like This
They Cannot Stay Like This

it tasted of sugar
in sour milk

I could bear to lick
but did not swallow

they say the best way to swim
is with your eyes shut

and a peg on your nose
can we eat together sometime?

maybe in your house
or not in your house

Utopia is a tiny place
that closes, see, it closes

and there are fruit machines
with only strawberries

I stuffed a few words
into my mouth

(leaves and grasses
leaves and grasses)

then spat them out
it was the best I could do

Prayer

I want to make some money
wear lace if I have to

The butter was left out again
and I can't bear to watch people

wrestling on beaches

when I want people to leave
I tell them I am going to sleep

and start making understatements
about melancholia

Sometimes I might have meat to cook
which can't wait.

I want people to stop
sending me photographs

They remind me of how peculiar mouths are

I'm a damp expanse, like a halibut
only halibut means 'sacred' and 'flat'

Real Sea

she is very normal looking
and she often peels a grape

to yell, look at my wet eyeball!

she can also be monumental
and smells good in a sheet

forgiveness tastes
like sunlit sand dunes

(says the cheerful book
but she knows better –

forgiveness tastes of thighs
and a spat out picnic)

people turn her on
like a monophonic radio

it's ok oh it's ok

she longs to slice a line
through thin blue canvas

she cannot be anybody's
mother today

Vagueness

like whether there are shadows
or a space

between the words

blouse, gnat, grip, core, lint, jelly, lulla

hey! does anybody know what wax smells of?
(digestive systems? paper hats?)

it took forever to think
of ferris-wheel for the crossword

nothing else fit

not even helter-skelter
which could have been perfect

the idea of a quilted beast
is poetic

lukewarm snow is water

because I opened
the screw top bottle

they cried
you've got great hands!

everything can always be another thing
– is that consoling?

Window

and no time at all
to wonder whether or not

a distinction between skin
and the flame out there

yes flames and the skin
or long brushed hair

and float our impeccable voices

CALLIE GARDNER

Callie Gardner's *naturally it is not*, published in 2018 by The 87 Press and excerpted in the present selection, is among the most ambitious and ground-breaking poetry books of the decade. Conceived as 'a poem in four letters' and composed over the course of a year, it 'challenges' (as Gardner puts it in an accompanying note) 'the (Western, Celtic) notion of the four-season wheel of the year' via an 'unnatural poetics' and utopian politics born of urban, queer life in the capitalocene. It's an exhilarating and trans-formative reading experience; on the page and in per-formance, every line sparks and shimmers with vivid potentialities of being. Alongside their editorship of *Zarf* magazine and Zarf Editions, and facilitation of the Poetry Circle at queer bookshop Category Is Books, Gardner's poetry presents a participatory reimagining of networks of form, body, community, text, world; its generosity and optimism are matched only by its daring and radical clarity of vision.

from springletter

                                                on this planet,
there are some soft guarantees when we consider
wishes and nature, the primary colours of debate
exclusionary in print, additive in the light show
and, in petrichoric pigmentation, sensitive to things' being
as dust. *And it is well to state*
that rain makes hills green / And the sky
blue and the clouds dark / And the water
water by them, but as we own, idiom
lands on both sides, encoding empire.
                                                blast windows
protect an insect colony comprising so many species
that there is no longer species, only individuals
and nuance. the children who come to beg
at the butterfly box decry this unrealistic practice:
biodiversity of (say) a tree gives no cue
for laddering the way up, shredding the bark
for functional biologies to proliferate in layers. nothing
less than lesson is crayoned approval: losing legs
makes the colony collapse to standing in the
face of criticism. *What is a utopia for?*
To make meaning. at the first interrational congress,
a paper of losing: manifesto of the *irréalisable*
(which is not to speak of lost in
lotus, but of easy pose marshalled with all
amicable might). the fruits of frequent subtheorising hold
every body is a utopia: unmobilisable force meets
an unmakeable object, and the deep resulting pore
of atopia is here to rain stopped play.
tangled together in their streets and sheets, delegates

pick significance out of each other's body hair,
reflecting on what's given: the presentation of yelling,
self-effacement in the facing basement of interpersonal noise;
a way to be together adapted into autonomies
proliferating under the sign of (attemptable, achievable) zone;
and *erotogenics intelligible* if only because the alternative
grinds us into cricket flour.

Italicised quotes from, in order of appearance:
Stein, *Stanzas in Meditation* (II:iii)
Barthes, *Roland Barthes*
Raha, *countersonnets*

from summerletter

no public / no republic
so much founded on the living room, coffee shop,
& museum

nothing to spend money on is the same as no money at all

vital in the slough
i want to look at the white sands and ogham
(this is where it's written, a qelticism)

where are the faeries-ferries and ethereal foxgloves
catching in the wind?
a snail with a car as its shell
here a slug on the path
here a vole
here a rabbit on the white sand
here a dog following bikes on the road
or a croaking bird on the rough isle

no justice no peace
while gilt and silver stand for nothing being regulated
and waves, voices, erroneous dust
cotton, silk, and ermine perfected
mine the tours

when the old dream of revolution shatters
into little ones of wealth (bad old story)
the domed horror is gold
indeed i think nothing is the same
that salvages two conventions twice

keep heavy metals coming out of the clouds
it's a baneful ideation on wry, bred
(or sprouted)
in the house of nuance, calendar dump
back up or down load

make it a mutinous sign or bound
everything that comes out between arches

this lochan is reed city
where are you rushing off to?
greed-furred geological fingers feeling blind
generative insights populating maps

england is now a dark green tunnel
of worry; is ever far-northernness a shield or shadowy
disguising cloak?
on this alien island so near its birth
every landscape collected in the magic-hour sun-rain
serendipitous beauty of birches –
the reeds grow like beards, like armpits,
like woven wet chests, like forgotten patches

these live and scatter themselves
against the cartographic crimelook
of the scrip na-multiplies, h-everything,
invisidhible consonthanants making the language thick,
ancient, and safe

all my tentacles

every fiber of our being is interlaced, even complicit, in the webs
of processes that must somehow be engaged and repatterned
  – donna haraway

a need now to see the insides
skin and flesh peeling off like
tentacular pages in probing strips
such is the sexless squid of the feels
no perspective on truth or an ocean's permanence
indeed no love is forever, so give that a go
old ones originally gather in chains, inspired
in chains, membranous, unarticulated but questing,
the simplest limbs probing this side or that,
the bad tool developed for the task even by revolution,
a formal requirement the brass need to tell what unfolds
from this new work, paid for out of mushroom-debt
rhizomatic finance questioned into things
and then the tentacle withdraws in sucking bliss –

another requirement: the geometric eye
and aquarious mouth of longing
cutting itself up about perspective
when we are walled up and given
no quarter in that process it engoldens
finding the gap turn from proper an exploding
star, ground blackly and backlit by dyes
i know there was no question
horizons wing it and count the solstice as
a shadow, where artificial justice persists

and subsides to the development of a line so far
an the archic itch for leadershit unfolds
and gathers speed in the folds.

even the simplest form will become only a facet
get centralised within benevolence. the stock of lives
makes meat a set and material a black mark
over the patterns of (admittedly assiduous) dust;
giving facts up over the time and date
there's need of acculturating open pods
which persist even as other insistencies go cold.
every form can't be an icon
but they can all be mutations in the depth-dark sea
no all divides but buds a perpetual pseudopod (again)
and this self-pure flesh begins to sing
event as it cuts itself open and gets wider
and more externally self-delighted

from please fall in love and leave me alone

1.

in macular crossing of sights,
the only two spots of discriminating void
where the contrast is in a readjusted ethics,
a treacly bloom somehow on a level
beyond seeing. flowers in the ontic,
they last emerge; how did they say
something so controversial yet so brave?

maybe you ARE that fruit,
capital-ash Æsthete, but still a bellicose datumn
insists on receptive recursion.
it's true, but you shouldn't say it.
silky *stricto sensu*, becoming-myriad
gives way to erosion fantasies,
to milky whitecaps past the corniches,

and, honestly? same. their public
booking of the hellish, aqueous
momentum is a graven image
and its selection a panegyric waltz,
an open distress against beauty,
down-at-home nebula modelling crisis.
thanks for coming to my ted talk.

5.

there can never be nothing cold – the floral black
enhances in its windy solitude the threshold
of harshness, thus expressed against the way
we now exist, in common cause with
well-worn unicorn appreciation (a happy gloss).
i weep willingly chopping an onion, knowing there's no
preservative dust like in the prechopped frozen kind.
small stones circle on the beach, henge enough for beltane,

and the latesummer stars give us a ziggurat,
calling-tower as much as we need and more.
it's roofed, and doesn't drop, perpetual-style
while all we say's inserted into song.
as a scribble face is somehow icon of a great
contribution, pawprint of a lion we'd never understand
in spanish or swahili, so conversation becomes,
under the present unsustainable conditions, government.

and so a swapped thought's a suzerain in the brain,
but still, there were many moments we do not
respire. turns out, a bad emerald's beryl veins
mutate, giving off poor satisfaction
when light aligns and limits plenitude.
sure, sunflowers look like they're paying attention,
but they just want that sweet vitamin d. don't let it become
another low tone from the wild bog, joining the redder night.

anaerobic dwellings live well to be maintained,
are their own masteries and subtle flings.
they stall themselves against philosophies,
take root and then dispel their heights and weights,
a deep relief we only feel when it's dry,
and hustle on through more eloquenter junes
until in panting, cancerous july
give up their shrivelled eaves to melody.

HARRY JOSEPHINE GILES

Harry Josephine Giles's work is motivated by protest, against structural systems of oppression and the pursuit of alternatives both pragmatic and utopian. What makes it so vital, and thrillingly so, is the ludic radicalism through which these alternatives are realised, with means including (but not limited to) Scots and minority languages, generative poetics and Twitter bots, live art and performance, punk rock and (with Darcy Leigh) their queer and trans DIY zine imprint Easter Road Press. Theirs is the rare trick of a process- and material-based poetics which remains resolutely participatory and outward-looking. Alongside their Forward First Collection Prize-nominated *Tonguit* (Stewed Rhubarb, 2016) and *The Games* (Out-Spoken Press, 2018), this spirit takes on a cosmic dazzle in the 'uncan wey of speaking, o pittan up wirds, / o wirkan, o haadan, o bidan' of the present selection, the opening sequence of *Deep Wheel Orcadia: a future fantasy* (Stewed Rhubarb).

from Deep Wheel Orcadia: a future fantasy

Astrid Docks

The chime o the tannoy is whit taks her back,
fer hid haesno chaenjed, nae more or the wirds
summonan her tae the airlock: her wirds,
at sheu haesno heard fer eyght geud year.

Sheu waatched the Wheel approch, gray-green,
tirlan fornent the yellow yotun,
pierheids trang wi yoles, wi glims,
an fund the gloup atween ootbye an in

gredually clossan – but only noo,
wi this soond, deus sheu ken whar sheu is.
The jaas o the transport appen, a gant
thrumman the bonns o the ship, a kord

whan the gangwey connecks. Astrid fingers
the saem o her sark, catchan een
an lukkan doon an tryan tae mynd
wha's uncan an whas naem sheu shoud mynd.

Sheu's browt a weyghty life on her back,
an whan sheu staps intae the airlock
sheu catches the doot o whit wad come
gin the pairts o her canno find thair piece.

The visietor, Darling, luks fer a piece tae bide

"J-Just to look," sheu says, catchan the poynt
o the yolewife's een. Darling, fer the first
time sheu's kent, habbers, o a sudden needan
tae explain hersel an no kennan hoo.
Sheu's raed aboot the Wrack-Hofn's mystery,
aboot the yoles landan thair haal o lights,
aboot the stoors in the gowden tide, aboot
the paece o distance, o fock at belang, aboot
a uncan wey o spaekan, o pittan up wirds,
o wirkan, o haadan, o bidan, an waantid tae luk.

"Ir ye noo?" says the wife, no askan,
her snackie haands deep in the wires o her craft.
"Ye'll be waantan tae spaek tae Eynar at the Hoose.
Hid's whit ye'd caa wir *bar*. He'll sort ye oot.
Tell him Margit sent ye." Fer Margit smells
sometheen aafil lik siller. Lik Eynar, sheu kens
the guff o neow traed. Sheu poynts the wey.
"Thank you so so much," says Darling. "I'm Darling."
Anither first: sheu blushes, seean Margit's
edge o smirk an hearan, "Is thoo noo."

Astrid sketches Orcadia

Sheu trails a finger ower her slaet in the curve
o her planet, then wi a canny swirl bleums
hids sweels o yellow an moorit broon. Wi shairp
stroks, the airms o Central Staetion skoot
atwart the screen, an peedie tigs an picks
mairk oot the eydent piers o Meginwick
in the corner o her careful composition.

An Astrid luks oot the vizzie-bell,
doon the tail o Hellay, kirk staetion,
the dammer o the Deep Wheel surroondan her,
an feels hersel faa, an lift, an faa.
Liv oot, sheu dights awey the natralism
fae her slaet, an stairts ower again,
abstrack, wi only the thowt o coman haem

but odd gittan wi seean no odds:
black lines fer the starns, blue dubs
fer the tides, green aircs for the peedie skail
o wheels an airms an bolas gaithered roond Central.
Sheu follows sense intae shap, an shap
intae color, an noo her slaet is closser
tae the grace ootbye, but closser maks more

o a ranyie. Again her liv. Again a blenk.
Astrid steeks her een an haads the device
tae her chest, lik her braethan wad lift Orcadia
tae hids surface. But the screen bides skarpy,
an the view bides stamagastan, an Astrid
sattles back tae waatch an braethe an mynd,
her fingers restan jeust abeun the slaet.

The pieces Darling's been

Fer her coman o age she asked o her faithers
a week's resiedential on Aald Eart.
Nae Ball, nae press confrence, nae giftid
Executiveship, nae ship, e'en,
tho aa her sibliengs haed taen the sleekest
o near-lightspeed racers. Thay narleens
imploded, but sheu haed inherieted airts
an negotiated the week in traed
fer a fill simmer o senior management.
Mars simmers is ower lang.

This wis the stairt o her travaigan.
Foo wi the guff o fifty-square mile
o aald equatorial rainforest, no
relandscaepid ava, sheu decided
sheu wadno gang haem, but see as muckle
o the seiven starns as sheu coud. Sheu peyed
a ecogaird tae mairk her doun
on the wrang manifest, an flew. She saa
the Natralist munka-hooses on Phobos,
whar papar refeused ony maet traeted

wi more or fire, praeched wershy beauty.
Sheu saa a demonstraetion staetion
o sepratist Angles: bred, snod,
rich, blond, an weel airmed.
Her faithers' credited wirds – first barman,
than teely, than dortan – trackid her
fae Europan federal mines tae stentless
pairties orbitan Wolf. Thay'd e'en
bowt time tae plea on the neow ansible.
At lang an at lent sheu tint them

on the ùnregistered Autonomist traeder
whar sheu teuk her neow naem
an body an face, whar sheu teuk time
tae choss an recover, at teuk her here
tae Orcadia, the innermost Nordren staetion,
eence the edge, eence the centre,
pangit an empie yet, an neow,
an eftir bletheran her rodd ower that
muckle a piece o space, lukkan
fer a peedie piece tae listen an luk.

Astrid meets the visietor, Darling

Astrid's sketchan the yoles at a pierheid on Central,
cosh in the neuk anunder a pilot light,
whan Darling snappers ower her, dingan
her styluses ower the deck o the vizzie-bell.
Thay waatch the gadjets hurl intae the clifts,
Darling spelderd ower Astrid's skirt.

Darling's apolojies an offers o credit
is as gabsie as Astrid's reassurance is blate.
"A wisno uissan them. Better ithoot."
Darling trys tae mak the fykie transietion
fae shock tae blether wi "Are you visiting too?"
an gars sometheen more precious gang.

But eftir, wi the offer o tea, Astrid gies
tae Darling whit sheu's waantan: lowsens the vooels
trow her spaekan, nods an smiles whan Darling
yatters on aboot community,
fills the visietor's lugs wi the neow aaldness
o her haem, blidelie spaeks whit sheu kens.

An eftir, eftir tea comes tae spirits, kennan
her ploys is watched by ivry lighter an grower
in the Hoose, chossan no tae mynd, seean
sheu's keepan back ower muckle fae Darling,
caran that sheu disno care, sheu leffs
at the dint o the invitaetion an follows the wumman.

Thair touchan's stammerie joy, trivvlan, agglan,
airtan, error, hixan, delight. The both
o thaim ken the meuvs an maan unlairn them
fer a neow skin's waas, windaes, doors.
Astrid taks a guff o Mars again,
an Darling o discovry. Thair tongs tak a gless.

Than eftir, whan the cruisies brighten tae morneen,
wi Darling yet sleepan, Astrid busks an luks
fae porthole tae bed, fae the tide tae Darling's hair,
an spiers o the gods, at dinno exist, gin
thir both fund whit thay waant, or need, or no,
or gin thir maed hid, or gin hid ivver maiters.

Darling an Astrid waatch a lightstoor

Darling is greetan. "I've never,"
sheu says, "I've never." An Astrid
kens the feeleen, but canno
decide, seean the stoor
o lights, the shaps thay mak,
the whips, the reid rivan
an gowd glisks, the skyran
dancers ower the bowe
o a roilan warld, the dillan,
the braeth, the lithy paece,
the dunt whan the planet-braid
linkwark o lights, togither,
sweys in a stark straik
ower the lip o sight,
whither o no tae say,
"Aye, but A mynd hid better.
Eence they wir more."

Astrid Docks

The chime of the tannoy is what brings her back, because it hasn't changed, no more than the words summoning her to the airlock: her words, which she hasn't heard for eight good years. She watched the Deep Wheel approach, grey-green, turntwistwhirlspinning againstbefore the yellow gas giant, pierheads fullactiveintimate with small boats, with points of light, and foundfelt the chasmcleft between outsidenear and in gradually closing – but not until now, with this sound, does she know where she is. The jaws of her transport open, a yawngasp thrumming the bones of the ship, a chord when the gangway connects. Astrid fingers the seam of her shirt, catching eyes and looking down and trying to rememberknowreflectwill who is a strangerweird and whose name she should rememberknowreflectwill. She has brought a heavymeaningful life on her back, and when she steps into the airlock, she begins to fear what will happen if the parts of her can't find their placedistancepart.

The visitor, Darling, looks for a place to stay

"Just to look," she says, catching the point of the yolewife's eyes. Darling, for the first time she's known, stammers, suddenly needing to explain herself and not knowing how. She has read about the wreck-havenharbour's mystery, about the small boats landing their haul of lights, about the stormstrifestrainspeeddust in the golden seatimetide, about the peace of distance, of folk who belong, about an unknownweird way of speaking, of praying, of working, of holding, of waitstayliving, and wanted to look. "Is that so?" says the woman, not asking, her cleverquickkindling hands deep in the wires of her craft. "You should speak to Eynar at the Hoose. It's what you'd call our bar. He'll help. Tell him Margit sent you." For Margit scenthuntsmells something very much like money. Like Eynar, she knows the stinkpuffsnortnonsense of new trade. She points the way. "Thank you so so much," says Darling, "I'm Darling." Another first: she blushes, seeing Magrit's edge of smile and hearing, "Is that so."

Astrid sketches Orcadia

She trails a finger over her multimedia composition and recording device in the curve of her planet, then with a skilledmagical flourishflounce blooms its waveswirls of yellow and redwool brown. With sharp strokes, the arms of Central Station jutthrust acrossover the screen, and little taptwitchteases and tapstrokespikes markscorefind out the constantindustrious piers of Meginwick in the corner of her careful composition. And Astrid looks out of the viewsurveystudyaiming-bubblebell, down at the end of the longest arm of Hellay, church station, the shockstunconfusion of the Deep Wheel surrounding her, and feels herself fall, and lifthelp, and fall. Palm flat, she brushswipes away the naturalism from her multimedia composition and recording device, and begins again, abstract, with only the thought of coming home and growing strangedifferent from seeing no difference: black lines for the stars, blue poolpuddlemuds for the seatimestides, green curvearcarches for the small scatterspreadspillleave of wheels and arms and bolas gathered round Central. She follows sense into shape, and shape into colour, and now her multimedia composition and recording device is closer to the gracceglory outsidenear, but closer makes more of a writhingpain. Again her palm. Again a blankblink. Astrid shutdarkens her eyes and holds the device to her chest, as if breathing would lift-bringhelp Orcadia to its surface. But the screen waitstaylives barethinbarren, and the viewstudysurveyaim waitstaylives bewildershockoverwhelming, so Astrid settles back to watch and rememberknowreflectwill, her fingers resting just above the multimedia composition and recording device.

The placesdistances Darling's been

For her coming of age she asked from her fathers a week's residential on Old Earth. No Ball, no press conference, no gifted Executiveship, no ship, even, though each of her siblings had taken the sleekest in near-lightspeed racers. They almost imploded, but she had inherited skillartdirectiongrift and negotiated the week in return for a full summer of senior management. Mars summers are very long. This was the start of her roamingramblingtravels. Drunkmad on the smellnonsense of fifty-square miles of oldoriginal equatorial rainforest, hardly relandscaped at all, she decided she wouldn't go home, but see as muchmore of the seven stars as she could. She payed an environmental quarantine agent to mark her down on the wrong manifest, and flewfled. She saw the Naturalist monasteries on Phobos, whose holies refused any foodmeat treated with more than fire, preached thinwatery beauty. She saw a demonstration station of separatist Angles: genetically selected, cleanabsolute, rich, blond, and well-armed. Her fathers' moneyedrespected words – first furious, then pleadingwheedling, then dismallonelystrangeraining – tracked her from federal mines on Europa to unrestrainedendless parties orbiting Wolf. They had even bought time on the new supralightspeed communication device. And long last she lost them on the autonomist trader where she took her new name and body and face, where she took time to choose and recover, which her here to Orcadia, the Northern station closest to the galactic centre, one the edge, once the centre, fullbursting and empty still, after locquaciously talking her way across such a big distance of space, looking for a small place to listen and look.

Astrid meets the visitor, Darling

Astrid is sketching the yoles at a pierhead on Central, snugquiethappyintimate in the nook under a pilot light, when Darling stumblestammers over her, knockdriving her styluses across the floor of the viewing-bubblebell. They watch the gadgets rolltumblespeed into the crackchinks, Darling spreadsplit over Astrid's lap. Darling's apologies and offers of credit are as voluble as Astrid's reassurance is shydiffident. "I wasn't using them. Better without." Darling tries to make the trickyrestless transition from shock to conversation and asks "Are you visiting too?" and makespushes something more precious go. But later, with the offer of tea, Astrid can perform for Darling what she wants: loosens the vowels through her speech, nods and smiles as Darling rambles about community, the community, fills the visitor's ears with the new oldness of her home, gladkindfondly tells her what she knows. And later, after tea becomes spirits, knowing her actionsdecisionsgames are watched by every lighter and grower in the House, choosing not to care, seeing she's held too much back from Darling, caring that she does not care, Astrid laughs at the shockchancestrike of the invitation and follows the woman. Their touch is stumblestammering joy, fumblefiddling, messdirtconfusion, searchfinding, error, laughhiccuping, delight. They both know the moves and mustshould unlearn them for a new skin's walls, windows, doors. Astrid smelltastes Mars again, and Darling, discovery. Their tongues take a drink. Then later, when the sun-lamps brighten to morning, with Darling still asleep, Astrid dressesprepares and lookpeeks from porthole to bed, from the seatimetide to Darling's hair, and asks of the gods, who does not exist, if they have both found what they want, or need, or not, or if they have created it, or if it ever matters.

Darling and Astrid watch a lightstorm

Darling is weepcrying. "I've never," she says, "I've never." And Astrid knows the feeling, but can't decide, seeing the stormstrifestrainspeeddust of lights, the shapes they make, the gustdarttwistattacks, the red wrenchripbreaking and gold glimpsegleampuffthrillscares, the shininggaudy dancers over the curveknot of a roiling world, the dimfadedieing, the breath, the lulling peace, the shockchancestrike as the planet-wide linkwork of lights, together, swerveswings in a thickviolent streak, over the edge of sight, whether or not to say, "Yes, but I rememberknowreflectwill it better. There used to be more."

COLIN
HERD

Since it's long been an empty platitude to describe a poet's work as 'playful' it is better, in Colin Herd's case, to go all-out and call it what it is: *fun*, and wildly, infectiously so. With four collections to his name, most recently 2017's *Click + Collect* (Boiler House Press), there is something irresistibly joyful about the elasticity and immediacy of Herd's line, redoubled by its shifts and metamorphoses and the queering, variegated abundance of his subjects – a spirit which also animates his pedagogy and online magazine *Adjacent Pineapple*. The pleasures of his work are akin to watching a friend's eyes light up when they talk of someone they love, or that sudden moment when we realise we're being watched and respond with both embarrassment and delight. It is by no measure a blandly 'happy' poetry – its compound notes of elegy, hesitancy, tension and doubt testify to that – but it is always resolutely, buoyantly, *alive*.

Kissed by Bubbles

Via a conversation with the brilliant poet
Erin Gannon, I found out about
Bubbles, persona of Anthony Torres,
from San Francisco, who was shot dead
in The Tenderloin in September 2017.
Bubbles was a House DJ, artist and activist,
whose work included Tranny Snow Cones,
churned out on the street from an
Italian Ice Cream Machine.

Bubbles pasted their tag all over the city,
a self-portrait with text saying:
shut up and dance.

Bubbles was a regular
(like the opposite of a fixture) at a dance night called
Housepitality. In a video for *The City Exposed*
by Mike Kepka in 2012, Bubbles said:
"Friends say that Bubbles is the fun me but
Bubbles is just like a character that I like to
go out as. It's fun. Bubbles is more like a toy.
… Bubbles is just Bubbles.
I feel empowered. The attention
is nice, I'm an attention whore, it
makes me feel important and loved…"

Bubbles' wardrobe included 60s flower print dresses,
ski goggles, long blond wigs (dreads, Heidi braids,
pig tails, Marilyn waves, Dusty Springfield hive,
you name it), shocking pink glasses,
shocking pink bra, bright yellow belt,

fade-change purple wig, polka bows,
denim jacket, multi-colour swimming
costume, multi-colour platform shoes,
hoop earrings, spangly studded hat,
Smiths T-shirt, red nose, Joy Division T-shirt,
Rolling Stones T-shirt, hoop earrings,
pink animal print handbag, purple and white
striped bikini, wobbly eye specs, cloud Y-fronts,
Mariachi hat, a pink phone,
silver hot pants,
space helmet, love heart sun glasses, beads, pearls,
tight blue jeans, fluffy pastel cardigan, huge blue
and fluorescent pink boots, silver and black swirl
leggings, black and white check prom dress,
tights in an array of colours and an
"The Artist is Broke" sweatshirt...

Bubbles ran a night called Sissy Bar.

One of Bubbles' artworks was a mixed media of
Marilyn Monroe blowing bubble gum.

Another of Bubbles' tag lines was
"Not the kind you blow. But you never know"
One of Bubbles' works is a Polaroid of them on a bed
with a mirror and underneath it says,
(very Magritte / very Mondrian / very Bas Jan Ader
if you ask me):
"This is Not a Line"

What I love about what I've seen of Bubbles'
art, and the way they spoke about it is
it's all fancy, all surface: no concept. The work
is strange, idiosyncratic, and
it refuses to solidify, refuses to singularise.

There are pictures of Bubbles made into digital mosaics
and all of Bubbles' work seems like
self portraiture as bubble-mosaic.
Bubbles like a lo-fi Akihiro Miwa.

There's a video on YouTube of Bubbles dancing at
a night called Stretch Sundays, at one point getting down
to do a kind of assisted shoulder stand
(hand stand-esque with someone holding their legs
in the air) and then they do some sexy press ups.

Talk-singing over a piece of music
released by Will Flat, Bubbles says: "I'm holding on
for dear life to San Francisco, the sub culture
they're trying to get rid of, it's still here…"
and

"there were clubs that used to open Thursday through
to Monday and on Monday the night was called Rehab"

and

"I used to get chased by the cops all the
time because of what I
was doing all the time"

Bubbles' Instagram is gorgeous.

There's a Barbie doll with Bubbles' handlebar moustache,
pictures of Bubbles with a "Frenchie from my flight home",
beautiful digital drawings in black ink,
posters for club nights, headdress pics, bulge pics,
boob pics, collages, anti-Nazi posters, outfits outfits
outfits, collages, berets, leather jackets, leggings,
lots of barbies, a nun filling up the screen wash of
a 4 x 4, masks, tights, a Miss Talent Sash, sun glasses,
shoes, loads of museum pop art, loads of homemade
pop art, sassy leg-crosses, early on a note saying "I would never
be a part of anything. I would never really belong
anywhere, and I knew it, and all my life would be
the same, trying to belong, and failing. Always
something would go wrong. I am a stranger and I
always will be, and after all I didn't really care",
Simpsons nail art, this whole series of pictures
of people on the street posing with the pink telephone,
its wire stretching out of the frame, lots of fags slipped
dangling out of Bubbles' mouth, a strange BMX phase,
and just so much more.

Bubbles' art is also all the tourist snapshots
of them in the streets, which must be diffuse,
lost, deleted. Bubbles grins or pouts in every one.
Bubbles hit local news in 2016 when they got ejected from a
bar because the bartender said the manager didn't like the
way they looked. In the SF Examiner, a friend says
"if Bubbles came to your party, you knew it was a fucking good party"

Bubbles would set up impromptu street discos with pop corn
as a kind of civic aesthetic duty... Paranoid London, who were
due to collaborate with Bubbles, have released a tribute EP,
The Boombox Affair, which uses vocals from a Facebook post
Bubbles made of breaking into a construction yard and holding
a solo rave. The track 'Beats and Bubbles' begins:
"This is what I brought and I'm playing my own records!"

The choice of Bubbles as a name seems utterly
perfect and utterly devastating – amorphous,
conjoining, beautiful, strange, surface... also
fragile and defiant to the max.

I get more from Bubbles'
insta than I do from *Spherologies.*

One artwork by Bubbles is a mirror written on
with pink and blue lipstick that says:

"you've been

kissed by Bubbles".

Weird Fight

My trousers were clumped
You asked if the fly was down
I said no
Then you went bananas

Fanciphobia

hello all of you
brilliant poets and poetry fans
such appetites etc
I was thinking
tomorrow morning
how about you
walk out of your jobs
and those without jobs walk into them
just up and toodle-ooo
just up and hello nice to meet you
take the staple gun
fantasize interiors
my name all of a sudden is
if you could redecorate
one thing
my name all of a sudden is
I want to quit my job
and start negotiating
(I like my job)
take the coffee machine
that's going nowhere
trellised rose wall-paper
take the watercooler
I'm so anti-it I can't put it into words
there's a kind of exit
that never really happens
that is just ongoing –
like saying all the time the whole party
I need to go soon I need to go soon

my lip is a hunk
my arm is
and people keep offering you stuff and
telling you stories
negotiate till doomsday
negotiate till kingdom come
indulgence is desperate
I'm such a flatterer
You are all so brilliant
You've written good poems
many of you have
I want to print out all your poems
and scrunch them up
and stuff them in my clothes
maybe read them first!
just maybe / no promises
my favourite Romantic poet is
Anna Laetitia Barbauld
I wear my fear around me
I fan it out on my pillow
and spray my pillow with it
I've never been moved by staff meetings
I hated *Call Me By Your Name*
except the conversation with a fish
and the clothes
the conversations with people
all through were so horrible
and then I watched it with someone who
hated it and I started to like it more
but *God's Own Country* I didn't have so

much beef with except the crouchy
wash was borrowed wholesale
from *Brokeback Mountain*
my name all of a sudden is Mark Kermode
good evening to you all
it's the audience that makes a performance
you are sleeping with stuff attached to you
you are car-less and sometimes annoying
but I don't hold that against you

Definitely wear trainers!

If everywhere was like Kenny Scharf's
Cosmic Cavern Closet, or better yet that we
didn't just glow in the dark but that we
actually changed shape, moulded like gum
to someone's shoe or someone's b-u-m.
I'm in this strange mood because
If anyone really cared
Oh I just can't get Up Helly Aa
out my head
I love a bar with dewdrops on the walls
I love a dewdrop on the forehead
Dewdrops in general are most satisfactory
a yellow dog made out
of bubble gum and it is the
exact opposite of Jeff Koons
the difference between blue tack and selotape is…
feels that way to me
serotype is a whole different sphere
I wish everywhere hubba'd + bubba'd
And everyone glopped and gushed
meant I could sink into {TBC}
meant I could be a part of
everyone treats you mean until
you let down their guard for them
and you do that by making a fool
of yourself but if you make too much
of a fool of yourself people start being mean again
{Continued} and you know what happens
to bubbles right?
They ju-ust flo-oat a-wa-y.

DAISY LAFARGE

The first four poems in this selection are from Daisy Lafarge's pamphlet *understudies for air* (Sad Press, 2017). It is an extraordinary sequence, the repetition of 'air' in each of its poems' titles alluding to musical airs and the pre-Socratic philosopher Anaximenes, who believed 'air' to be the universal substance from which all being is shaped. Both these resonances amplify a key characteristic of Lafarge's poetry: a dispersal of the lyric-I into the world which constitutes it, 'empty / but imbued with residual function', wherein signs are less conduits of meaning than impression, upon speaker and reader alike, and which nudge us, provisionally, towards radically ecological modes of thought. Her crossovers into visual art practice and work with MAP Magazine further exemplify this approach, and as the airs give way to 'capriccio' – more 'fauvist' but nevertheless 'partially obscured' – so Lafarge's poetry continues to present vital ontological alternatives to our anthropocentric complacency.

falsification air

what can I pass on, you ask,
about methods of detecting the air?
it has become so habitual
I am not sure where to begin.
each morning I walk into the world
looking for signs. early, before light
is normalised by the shadow of buildings
and the gentle fraying of traffic. it seems the signs
are most attracted to states of dereliction.
to receive them, it helps to be empty
but imbued with residual function
like a disused water tower
or any number of withering technologies.
lie back. let the world grow over you
like weeds. consider the sheets of air
gridlocked in double glazing. now
are you beginning to understand?

driftwood air

if a body collects meaning
the way driftwood girds
a beach with a periapt
of scum, then
that morning, we found some.
I preferred the thigh-
sized lengths of greening
torsion, thick and bunioned
with sea-tied knots.
they closed in my hand
like eyes. in the bay's centre you
found a log and deliberated
how to get it back on the boat, without
us sinking. *I could stay?* but you shook
your head, as if you'd already
weighed us up, said *A good haul today.*
we pushed off, watched
the land shrink to pigment.
often, there is no driftwood
for months at a stretch. even at dawn,
you find the beach already gleaned
or reclaimed by the tide.
some dawns, you said,
can last for years

aggregate air

what immunity for
buildings against their
uprooting; city skins
grown thick with corporate
heraldry, scabbing the air
tight to wound. on every corner a tree
articulates its script, whole flyovers
cracked with growing pains.
for a short while we considered
talking cures: a vernacular for pipelines,
circuitry, the fetid grids and systems.
we soiled our mouths to mimic
the good fettle of root and seed.
waited quietly for the rains

eclosion air

the husks were everywhere, but still no one knew
what they were supposed to have emerged
from. the world had fallen from its pedestal,
and in its place left a globular question
around what had always been. the question
shimmered, gave off a scent of sulphur, and
could only be approached at ecliptic conjunctions
of two or more bright objects. some things
stayed the same: the smell of cordite, shadows
of hands dancing over coffee tables, the walk-of-shame
lino in staff kitchens, the smutting of dun-colour set
into pavements, as if the asphalt were filled with seeds.
you could even look someone in the eyes
and tell them, as before, 'I love you', but the words
would breach in the air between, haplessly
smearing the root

from capriccio

I slept through the season of dogmatic awakening.

The wind sung through our victuals.

You found yourself adrift in the straits of the year.

The mystic on the hillside scours her sacred rocks.

I wait patiently for texts to become overripe and fall from branches.

The ground agog with fleshy lozenges.

A rare sentiment appears, goes to seed, is gone.

Parts of the body etiolate.

A text that you wanted – didn't want – to arrive, arrives.

The announcement of pleasure is muffled.

A woman saunters in chamois leather, limbs tacky from
convected heat.

In cosmic genealogy, the ocean is surrounded by a circular
mountain wall.

A daughter marks the horizontal limit.

Mental bed frames stretch along the where and why axis.

On December 3rd I was congratulated for drinking a stylised espresso on a Poussinesque bridge.

I did not drink yet the memory scalds.

Pines point their cones up then drop them like anchors.

A wood might be a cloister of sacrilege, or sacrilege, cloistered.

When I began to experience pleasure I no longer understood who I was.

A door with a curtain on both sides.

Half an apse – as if cut with a cheese wire – three brown brogues, two black, a Christmas wreath and a fistful of candles, arrange themselves in a landscape.

In the trompe l'œil city, at the moment of seeing the wood for the trees, citizens are habitually 'disappeared', leaving rumpled piles of clothing in the streets, one or two shoes.

I know where I'd rather beatify.

Rare juniper disease depreciates the gin market.

You advance towards tesserae of zucchini.

A breakfast of liquids and solids, everything labelled 'muscle milk'.

Tinsel tied around my waist, thighs, wrists, neck – a tail left at the nape, slack noose.

A fauvist messiah plays the violin, facing a page of partially obscured sheet music.

Dusk pink roses fall to create a framing effect.

Many women with dark curly hair.

A woman with dark curly hair smiles at the camera.

A woman with dark curly hair stands with one leg up showing tattoos of blurry handwriting on her thigh and wrists.

A woman with a face without a single line, just colour and shadow.

A woman seated with a double bass.

Side-on view of a woman with blonde curly hair, soft pink top like petit filous, a clock in the background telling quarter to six.

A woman with wavy brown-blonde hair, tired smile, taut eyes.

A biro drawing of a woman with curly hair, chin pulled up and back as if by a bridle.

Superman flies over the Château de Vaux-le-Vicomte, the sky is cyan and unremarkable.

I wanted, didn't want.

Is this what you imagined?

NICKY MELVILLE

nicky melville (aka nick-e melville) has been working at the forefront of experimental poetry in Scotland for over a decade, taking his cues from poets such as Tom Leonard and Ian Hamilton Finlay, and applying them with a typographical precision and guttural vengeance to the linguistic detritus of the neoliberal age. Best defined (in an anagrammatic fortuity that speaks to both his poetics and his east coast upbringing) as an 'avant-radge', his work can be found everywhere from small presses to international anthologies. Of particular note are his 2010 collection *selections and dissections* (Otoliths), 2014 poster poem *me* (Unit 4 Art), 2017's *ABBODIES* (Sad Press), and the as yet unpublished (but available online) *The Imperative Commands*, a 365-page process-found-poem of unparalleled scale and ambition. As the present selection demonstrates, whether in a concrete or lyric mode (or somewhere in-between), Melville's work is the correction fluid to the corrupted food of our austere and precarious existences.

sent.ence
1

an expression of natural language

stanza [orc raft]

lines forming
a unit
of verse

too far[5]

if you don't take things
too far
you don't know
how far
you can take things

too far
how far
you don't know
you can take things
if you don't take things

you don't know
how far
you can take things
if you don't take things
too far

how far
you don't know
you can take things
too far
if you don't take things

you can take things
too far
if you don't take things
how far
you don't know

from Poems, Chiefly Tipp-Exed

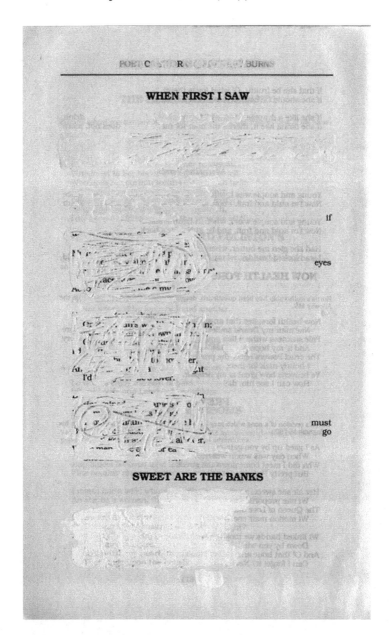

POE C   R   BURNS

WHEN FIRST I SAW

if

eyes

I'd

must
go

SWEET ARE THE BANKS

before

OPEN THE DOOR TO ME

corpse

end times   of the month, November 2018[1]

I have two pound in change
well   a two pound coin
which Anne Laure gave me
this morning
but I need change
for the bus
      which is the reason
      I asked her for it
which is one pound seventy
so   I can buy some rizlas
which are 29p from Tesco
I will go to Willie at the checkout

I have two pound left
on one of my credit cards
      can't use the other in shops
      as I can't mind the pin
      but there's nothing in
      that one either
I can use that for lunch
I'll buy a croissant
and a boost
      give your self a boost
they only have boost duos
      give your self two boosts
in this Tesco
though they feel as if
they're not full size

---

1. Well, it could be *any* fucking month, or sometimes
any *part* of the month, to be honest.

but it'll still work
the croissant is 79p
the sweet 85
I'll buy these
      get boosted
at the electronic cashier
even though I'm against them
cause I'm too embarrassed
to go back to Willie
even though he's probably
more damaged than me
            maybe I am more damaged than him[2]
I know he has epilepsy
I remember him from school
he's slightly older
I wonder
what else
has happened
since I saw him have a fit
playing rubgy
      I fucking hate rugby
      why did I have no agency
      as a teenager
      I know why

---

2. This is a nice line, shows a lot of craft. 'I am' is a pun on iamb / and can be read
   as one. '[M]aybe' may be a two stressed, like me, spondee. Thus spondee iamb
   iamb anapaest. Or it may be a trochaic *maybe*. That could then lead the iamb
   'I am' / to read as a trochaic *I* am [Two hypercatalectic lines there (maybe)].
   Maybe may be an iambic may*be*. However [amphibrach] / that stress pattern
   sounds a bit weird / but might be nice to recite.

Willie looks seriously
medicated almost
lobotomised
    what a life
he's probably got more
money than me though

one final problem remains
for today
I said I'd make soup
butternut squash
to use up the veg
in the veg box
but we need bread
I have 60p left in the bank
might be able to get
a half baguette
with that

I get these helpful banking texts[3]

Saturday 17 Nov • 12:03

thanks for the input
Bank of Scotland
if I had enough
to cover payments
it would be banked

A/C 9348 17Nov. Your overnight
balance was £20.60. As this is near
your limit, please ensure you have
enough money in your account to cover
any payments.

there's no magic money tree
unless it's Quantitative Easing
which is not for me

_____

3. A simple way to stay on top of your finances without
   even having to think about it. Except you do.

withdrew the last twenty
quid at the weekend

that 60p
is the same one
I just mentioned
for the bread

I want to at least pretend
I have some dignity left
by not asking Anne Laure
to get the bread[4]

I'll go to Sainsbury's near me
when I leave here
the bakery
at the Tesco
isn't working at the moment

I eat both boosts
didn't intend to
there's something wrong
with me
I'm too thin

the croissant's not very nice
though quite buttery
bit dry

---

4. Massive fail. Also asked for something sweet, unlike
   me, and some baccy cause I just ran out.

the super market

very little helps

corpoem one

IAIN
MORRISON

'Sapphohabbies' perfectly encapsulates the unique and exhilarating experience of reading an Iain Morrison poem. Delighting in the musicality of language, tender and conversational, it finds its 'revenge' against violence and hatred in the most festive and life-affirming 'stand a-love', while Morrison's use of the Sapphic stanza to queer the Burns 'habbie' stanza – a kind of drag at the level of poetic form – renders this affirmation in the very fabric of his craft. The same spirit is in evidence in his performances (among them hosting a night of drag queen poetry, and a durational installation in which he read aloud every Emily Dickinson poem) and in his first collection *I'm a Pretty Circler* (Vagabond Voices, 2018). As it 'creates community not just content', so Morrison's poetry is among the most valuable – not to mention contagious and convivial – being written today, a product of his uncommon and consummate blend of experiment and candour.

Don'cha Don'cha

Do you think you
won't die tonight

Screaming as it seems
is ultimate in death after all

You lived abroad before
to experience that loosening

Firing self
up in a ready room overlooking

To pilot empowerments
in Edinburgh

Sapphohabbies

Qu-qu, Qu-qu, Qu-qu-qu, Qu-qu, Qu-qu
Ee-ee, Ee-ee, Ee-ee-ee, Ee-ee, Ee-ee
Rr-rr, Rr-rr, Rr-rr-rr, Rr-rr, Rr-rr
      D-d-d, D-d
i-I, i-I, i-I, i-I-i
a-A, a-A, a-A, a-A-a
rr-Rr, rr-Rr, rr-Rr, rr-Rr-rr
      y-Y, y-Y
mm-Mm, mm-Mm, mm-Mm, mm-Mm-mm
      ee-Ee, ee-Ee.

Think I'm having one of eureka moments?
Your affective take on my first engagement
reads me worst when most it neglects our variant
      modes of expression.
An habit of financial ruin
sees what it opts to see, not heeding
the drag from food or buy-to-let when
      the banks stayed cashed.
Deleveraged, though, reduced commitments
      make gloomy graphs:

how a foot has stood on 2016!
Euro boost we're getting, mind you's surprised
with
modest growth apparent across the quarter,
      Russia is shrinking.

A couple of percent's a pain for
exporters stuck at bottom levels,
their cloth is stretched. You'll note the current
        account its weakest,
the worst it's been, if not yet held as
        a stress position.

Output, productivity, what's the difference?
Figured man confronted with daunting noughts, I
felt this morning, moving through airport systems,
        filled with flat lines,
a clouding I wished unconnected
to those in air we somehow met
and swallowed as they lined the skies of
        our aircraft's flightpath,
the trans Brazilian dead, returning
        as apparitions.

Ana Matheus steadily had been posting
as their number neared to two hundred women
killed last year. I broke up my hour and half flight
        mentally adding
as more than one per minute flew through
the tube our storage lockers made them.
We'd only hear their bundled forms as
        they thumped above,
and tense, sure that the doors would open
        in bursts of clothing.

Only forty seconds or so between the
body hurtles, we wondered dimly how our
luggage passed them; still the illusion somehow
        encapsulated
each phantomed body, onetime real.
Exquisite corpse of our reviews
we wondered whether we'd join up
        in what we asked.
Being the cis male respondent
        I felt pushed back.

Mirror, mirror, what would you wish me mirror?
Spoken to as man that's a zero presence,
from the start confess the desire that her book
        alters in writing.
The stage door to the Fringe is open.
I host a play, *Picasso's Women.*
For two weeks actor Colette Redgrave
        and her star Judith
and her star Kirsten strut performing
        their scripted speeches

penned by Brian McAvera, first performed at
National Theatre, Radio 3 conjointly,
Russian Olga, Marie-Thérèse and Fernande
        barter acceptance.
Considers what are right dynamics
of powered men and their relations
to women in the current context,
        a thoughtful play,
so add it to your August list
        and don't delay.

Iain Morris' debut collection *I'm a*
Pretty Circler, tender within its pages
punchy, patterned poems with drag queens in them
    £9.95.
Has also lived and worked in Cambridge,
responsibly commissions poets,
and for the first time you return him
    a book he sold,
which bids him swell on straight mechanics
    of text reception.

Houses stretch their girls on the runway, marking
where your queer security's strained and strengthened.
Love and perspiration, our fight is foursquare,
    here's where it shows
in time, in money, children being
like me anthologised, moreover
I'm read in Orkney, I have photos
    to prove Brazil
and haply by departed loved ones
    in heaven still.

Here's my thought how writing or readings of it
makes, creates community not just content,
read by some, by breathing is spread to others
    out through the stirred world.
Per conta da sensibilidade
An inflammation of the ear
has caused a sensitivity
    that's meant these last days
I go to sleep while listening to
    the pulse my heart beats.

This same inflammation resulted from a
targeted assault on my life. The picture
shows me here in hospital two days after,
        late in November.
With luck recovery continues
and this is my part-healed appearance.
I share the story with you grateful
        we lost not this one,
and stand a-love, a sister put it,
        our best revenge.

Ha-ha, Ha-ha, Ha-ha-ha, Ha-ha, Ha-ha
A-a, A-a, A-a-a, A-a, A-a
Pp-pp, Pp-pp, Pp-pp-pp, Pp-pp, Pp-pp
        Y-y-y, Y-y
nn-Nn, nn-Nn, nn-Nn, nn-Nn-nn
ew-Ew, ew-Ew, ew-Ew, ew-Ew-ew
y-Y, y-Y, y-Y, y-Y-y
        ee-Ee, ee-Ee-ee
a-A, a-A, a-A, a-A-a
        rr-Rr, rr-Rr-rr.

Jan. 2019

Blarney/Soosage/SoundEye

Who's next people?
Come round now
anyone
watch yourself
next
the girl on the stone
who's next?
Come through
lie back
no bags
yes I'll take a photo for you
put yr head back
right back
hold onto the bars
head back
slide down
lower now
down lower
lower
further
and kiss
good man
up you come
mind your bag
I took quite a few
who's next now
to the stone?

The Huff, the Stand-off, the Counter-huff

Huffy with Alice over the milk
Jo blew steam from her hot black tea.
Alice, soon in the huff herself
with silent Jo, called Steven a name.
Furious Steven, an amplification of huff,
plunked himself down to moan to Gregor his pal.
Gregor explained Alice was just peeved
at the silent treatment from Jo.
Steven, calmed, didn't take time to thank Gregor
who, mildly riled, stepped out for a walk
and in five minutes wavering
the small hurt had gone away.

Home, Gregor hugged Jo, they talked –
Gregor had the best chat. Jo changed.

Jo sent a text to Alice making things up
and relaxed on the couch.
Alice was round at the shop when Jo's text came.
By chance, Steven was too; unmindful Alice
patted his back in the queue
as Steven bought a litre of milk
and Gregor's favourite pizza.
This, all of the housemates shared,
arranged in the living room later
in front of RuPaul's Drag Race,
entertained by the drama
and all of the fierce queens' antics.

Farben *(after Schoenberg)*

Farben Farben Farben
The sound colour
rubbing words like
coming against each other
Chord timnal, orb, humnal
what the publisher says when
the publisher says
You should call this
        Summer Morning by a Lake
you sink down a little

harmony's smidgeon and blur
bludgeon and shusher,
umurgence, these paintings
        no lines judge
   tonic sounds which seem unbalanced
that oboe though

—

contemporary trauma
the subject matter that is just,
just not there
undeniably shades
in on
        the inward figure
an instrumentalist plays accurately

What comfort us?
us it is possible
for aluminium methodologies
to stutter, bask, stutter

which pitches inward
            with that kind of logic
the conductor's pulse pulse

—

pulse is phenomenal
            tonal depression
of the impending colour stage
yellows, greens, browns,
pinks blown and images
pulse pulse

that sound-a-like colour
coming to
the prescribed dynamic
according to the nature of their
    instruments.

—

There are no motives in this piece
        which have to be brought to the fore
Klang Farben Farben amassing
thus is still less convoluted

what we call forms
evokes and affect
Then it must
the evaluation of colour in tone
be possible
        has been graven

NAT RAHA

Nat Raha's poetry, as the title of her most recent collection *of sirens, body & faultlines* (Boiler House Press, 2018) suggests, is one of finding fissures in the 'given' channels of language and dynamiting the moribund fuck out of them. Not for its own sake (though the destructive relish with which her work meets conventional syntax is positively rapturous), but as a making of noise and an assertion of presence against a world which would prefer to make voices like hers inaudible, invisible. As such, it can be read as an extension of Raha's queer and trans activism; she works with various local and international collectives and edits *Radical Transfeminism* zine, among other activities. Her work in performance is likewise explosive, with Raha often using a loop pedal to render those 'faultlines' with visceral intensity. To call her poetry a radical gesture fails to do it justice; it is radical in every fibre of its being.

sonnet,

                                        joy graze the tones of you.
        heads hail to fixtures we split daily at foundation, translates light
        to pleasure
                        gaping
                        turns perception.

                                        slow electrics / dissolve guilt
                        its press hours on your temples–
                        kept flown by the city itself:

            how the find & glass of each
            postcode will fascinate , refract affect
                                        / heat haze pry
        that this always will be of politic,
                                        unless we can swap breaths
        w/out one part NO_x
                        not the silver gelatine still as we
                        age depth by vibration–
                                to place the aural sculpt always further
                or what we do not, etches
                                        kept for self-relic
                told in gestures, necessitates the days pulse

(sonnet)

takes what fleshtones from our
kelp & ink split on dark
eyes & washed in the hers
-tory of desiring.
                              calves
solo bare ramparts
: raw metropole's foreclosures,
greyed.

                    if yous compelled
   by directives & gives
   up on queer love ,

      in these next night returns
         (or jet to it, prosper!)
   onto our declining hands
   cold as cuts the astronomical light

... freeze in the dream stock ,
slid beyond best & taken freely
to tongues,, this

larder open to all who would stum
-ble, invitation to feast. we took

road beside the hill, regency cut-off
spoke its news to all encountered, evening light
takes the day's heat edge, & round—

cut to glass walkway, footfall quell the
distance of the police barricade
, leith,, tarmac, armour, slow smoke up
-surge scene on mute / more
talk with the passing, discern
this below

: you, who I do not yet know
bejewelled
, tall juxt. to dark hair the light
hits heels yours as the police
charge the barricade beneath, smoke dou-
sing scene / fear for
the glass in the horse
charge. this canteen
belonging to students,, dive
into lift / though i block
departure to give/ask a name, voices

dropped. door crash against my frame, dark
a red jacket. take turn on these
mechanics, liberating what foods for the flesh

[15 july 18]

our / intensive support *

> to be open towards / for
> healing , tinged negative

>   cacophony
> salutations rub / skid / through
> breaking , that we could be
> this warmed

> our intensive valuations &
> graze / manifest, slips
> out of narrations & herstory , tense
> rips the nuance from our throats
> close to cognitives //
> converse song of possible
> shifting of possible arms &
>   syntax , *arms of miraculous refusal*
>   bare corporeal

> how we feel through the particu-
> larities of our brokenness / its
> worth possibly together

here in the diaspora, un-
learning faux cultures
                    , their
investments in our arms & genders

                    / our solidarities
                    vicious, damaged,

          heinous / educators & the registration of citizens ,
          directs the promise / possible
          ─/ refuse to answer
          a poetics of violent
                    & good nationhood ⧣

frustrations & sourced / we
                    overwhelmed w/ healing
                    & waged work
plotted a sequence of perverse beauties, our commoning :
                    a conception of need they could not
                    grasp.

                    of our bruises
                    & collective selves ;; fabrications
                    of / consciousness
                    the care that grows
                              us together, yet the
                    glamour & fracture of such love
                    scarce / down the

from [9x9]

[1]
this of obscure cosmos / violence
daily reiterated, purged
vivid, paused blood in fire & syn
thetics << silver & liquid
eyes stencilled brick quot
-as / authors who could not
conceive us & hold / to have live

-d im/possible gravity „
chilled & // all known ways

[2]
decimate, un/made & horny
, our shaven flesh & locks, dined on
black beans, corn & sugar, *vagabonds,*
tinkers, tricksters & jailbirds <
had demanded our bodies o
fascist rags, codes & division
s systematic flesh & capitals

nostalgia imposed & gen
der/ivative nations „ soil *f≈*

[3]
agree: your logic treacherous [#]
political & philosophic senses
,, distribution of thought & activ
-ity engineer'd [#] divest
meant hot policing & exot
-ic / *but some of us want to keep*

our jobs" in yur demand that we flesh
nice for pills & being / had
abolished yur entitlements,, our

[4]
sexes & flesh constituted
from the women & femmes who charged

you: pale & sweating majorities /
pathetic smears & intonations
assured & arrogant thieves f$
if your violence is a source of pleasure
/ we trust our anxious days & juts
where once bridges, borders, declining

winter bones;; keep gorgeous, keep warm

[5]
grrrl // if we are citizens
of nowhere, a threat to the tone &
image;; composed / lace cute
we divine femmes no here to dissect
your impositions >> bark organs
so late in the day, directions
on casual violence: if your pleasure
excruciate living / &
the beauty about our eyelines

[6]
these decades old violence, for board
stars & black salt, she said the possi-
ble diminished / order admini
stirred names, ~~// norm~~

haar & solstice eyed / fall into
the waged day , turbulent shimmer
out of discourse traded close, pinned
/ ordinary trappings & verse
to squat ,, dis / locate

[7]
in nationhood, your reveries
five hundred truncated years, we
dined on stolen whisky, tar, minis
-terial bones / forced to find work
a rustic allegory, regen-
narrating cities & ag/gressions
light & nature false con
dition'd : cohered by skins our
≠ separated, crashed ~~i in~~

[8]
at the trial of yur crimes of invention
in my charred golden minidress /
cremated homes, debt && circuits
capital commission & hate

dined on flour, divine salt &&
threads of your flags ,, aroused,
our vulgar comedy, drives &
erotics silenced >/ ~~your~~ beliefs
& rituals :: disintegrating, foxed

[9]
[≈] we impossible siblings,, lobes
sore, close hairs & gleaming / our
traumas dismissed / bitter salt stream
-ing cheeks, spark / structurally

yur lavish/ious divisions
& devaluations, institut
-ions, blood,, harmonics, assembly
of work, migration & con
jugal / flicker, track memory

MARIA
SLEDMERE

Maria Sledmere's poetry exists at the blurry thresh-
olds between real and virtual, sense and memory,
subject and object. Following an epithet for *SPAM*
with whom Sledmere is Poetry/Nonfiction Editor, it
is a 'post-internet poetry', born at once in the shifting
imaginary strata of our networked existences and the
collapse of ecological 'reality': the aporia of a future-
projected arcadia and the crisis of its non-realisation
in the digitised present. Sledmere's work comprises
a compelling cross-pollination of blogging, criticism,
music journalism, collaborations with artists and
musicians such as Lanark Artefax, work with *Gilded
Dirt* magazine and A+E Collective and a new editorial
role at Dostoyevsky Wannabe, alongside her 2018
pamphlet *Existential Stationary* (SPAM Press) and
nature sounds without nature sounds (2019, Sad Press).
The result is an intoxicatingly disruptive poetics of
the 'plaza': those interstitial spaces of late capitalism
where nostalgia, pleasure and fantasy commingle
with anomie and a diffuse sense of dread.

Object Sheltering

these concrete encryptions
    softly speak to me, the little detonations
        of silky asphalt   argent in rain
            less of parlet than starving, hardened

the event of the thing

                            an extinct bliss

                                miss misery of the poppyseed

            tainted daisy

                                these unsettled staves

is ever a mouse click pride of regret
of browser alignment, lift

                inside light as light is confinement

    to fetishise dark skies

                                            to feed off reason,
                                                breathing
                                            uneasy for sleep, stolen
                                                    his manner

a littoral bleed into green, brine, miasmic night

and so loved one, you come to me now out of silence
you are messenger blue and anonymous to others
biding our time in velvet fullness, however

as ever

it looks: plenitude
recedes

to a strangeness of strangeness
if this would fold, lisp then twist like a leaf
i would love better his lilac eyes, a virgo's depth of emotion
one cannot form as with salt or clay
what emits or gorges, fleshes to memory

important to drink while the sun's still okay
or trauma remains as undissolved thought
bubbling the milk of the stomach, an advert in blue
retains null exception (i miss you, i miss you)

we don't know the contours

we drink

                  inside seashells, honing
the opalescence of inverted whisky
                        comes slick as a promise

                                          from lovelorn lips

                              to penetrate / rent / to send one over
a core blooms   too easy the furore of mourning

            liquidity, quicksilver, singing
                        the undone gossamer hum

comes toward dawn   is easy   lucky   free   (maybe)
      a luxury bristles, syringes the silt of the sea
                  till ever metallic backed down and feeling
            navy, gracious, a pear cut in two by the sun
in slant light, gold effect razors   the age from me
insidious debris of five-fingered glory   ranged   arras
      the arras arranged   space being rumour of old mentality
            cash flow depictions   assembling slowly
/ i become past on the ore [oil] of thorax

is it spicy, a lifeline cast to new ether
or formless, a wrapping of cellophane
            gleaming theme
/ apropos of death i feel nothing
except hangover dreams
   on familiar carpets, smelling dust as the skin of each love
inside a quiet wanting   magpie & jewelline quantity of meaning
               rouses a knell   that is cyclone lively, prone to repeat
                    the wild   .

                         in me   in me

(((
      )))   .

Ayr/Air

The sound was shrill and it tasted like the seaside in my ear
and it gave me indigestion, just thinking about it
like when we were teenagers always just living off five-packs
of supermarket bakery cookies
and the police would move us
and the staff would move us
and the woman who served the coffee would ask us to leave
and we found shelter in doorways
not from the rain
and sugar was our conduit to a better future
because we needed energy to get around
and move between places
with the howl of the wind in the dunes forever
licking dust off our fingers.

Diana

On a cerulean loveseat, you counterfeit dreams to the analyst;
the impress of your body makes clouds on fabric.
He was in me, we slept three times
and saw a rabbit strung from a lamp post
the noticing crowds of chanterelles.
Not the same howl, but equalised trash in measure.
Relax, redact this. Toothpaste takes care of it;
nicely, whitely. As he speaks
you pick off flakes of synthetic ocean
and murmur the seven plus colours of rainbow;
under your breath is a furious jewel,
which you pluck at the end, in lieu of a cheque.
There are these spores all over the future.
After the appointment, starlight sounds different
upon human skin; it is far more minor
and you sense distance, brushing the ivory
for cooler erasures, monsoon season.
Supine, you confect letters to financiers
in Russia, America. You have seen
the order of everything, the hunger of water.
If only you could swim with dolphins here.
You lack sufficient spit for a stamp.

Milkies

The wonderful room had a galaxy quality. I could work out how
to adjust the volume accordingly, so there was just all this matter,
and a sort of tarry blackness I chalked up to loss. We were in the
room feeling planetary, tracing ariadne's thread, and kissing each
other's digits for warmth. There were so many thrilling notifi-
cations, until there were none. The chocolate would melt on the
sill without sky, and liquid you would rise up through the carpet
like a sort of moss I could lie on. This is not the grief they told
me I would experience. Nothing could prepare my body for the
aquamarine downpour, nor the disappointment of finding my
belly full of starry wasps, not stars. They glitched and flickered
out of existence, and remember the universe requires a fall to
continue. Something rolls away. I'm not saying it simply hurt. Is
there a crack inside a crack in the sky, which we can't see from
the window. Nightly I have all these dreams of the station. Fair
Isle, Leuchars, softest blue. Whenever you pulled the lights out
my hair I would feel an inward crumple, like somebody faraway
just taking a dress off. Everything is happening in a kodachrome
video, which runs back and forth in the judder of a list of
ingredients. It is a kind of gelatine, it is forbidden. We cannot
fix it. The necessary silk was synthesised, and we ran out on the
tarmac to adorn its surface, and all of the lies came out of us, fell
upon dirt in packets of white. The raindrops were bigger than
marbles; they were whole bright words. We named them milkies
and slipped some into the lies. You scooped the rest up and held
them in your mouth, until everything about you was entirely
glass, opalescent, and perfect for the menagerie which my mother
had prepared for us. Luminaries came in, and redacted our eyes.
We were ornamental, and settled. We knew that elsewhere, some-
one was giving birth to us.

A Charmed Life*
For Scott Hutchison

There's a lore in the unsung morning
which you chose to sing
We didn't need these things, these things
forgive me

The loaded emotion in weekday smoulders
a soft fringe of language, where here the salt roar
comes over you, slowly

Splits across Scotland a scar
of complicated sorrow, Firth of Forth, such slosh
and debris of unseen feeling

I could hardly believe the news in its happening
refreshing each page right through the night
until the next chorus

This hurt like a shipwreck
splintering against our showers of avatars
So what throbbed in Selkirk, over and over
the sober rush into static

This lovely May which feels wrong, its blush
of blossom and sun, eye and aye
a bright blue dawn
which you missed at midnight; a long time gone
yet half as long

---

* A message Scott sent to a friend, just weeks before his death: 'But then, what have we
got to be complaining about? Plenty, privately. But really, it's a charmed life.'

I cannot fathom, looking for a western sky
and a shire of mine
There's a friend in the dark who knows you
and a thousand more online, in the air

If only you could see the warmth in these stories
Can you hear, can you hear our voices?

What belongs when you say it, graceful
and away now, shyest
between the North Sea and the North Atlantic
I make of this place dear green, dear breezeblock
and tender concrete, the sweetness of youth's
ever suffering stopped

In that second, or else the hours before the hours
I'm watching you watching the water
as you watched before you leapt

And there's gold out there, the carbonated raise
which froths at the top and stills by a football moon
I'm kicked in the cunt of your beautiful lyrics
I mean love among brokenness
I mean you left too soon

Behind this architecture of empathy
every lost sketch is a promise
that any day or year, looking in the black
and blue for answers, you stepped
from the noise of the dance, never seen again
but heard, but heard.

For Winter Solstice

Consider my plagiarised landscapes, the slow curve
that brings us back to blue. If we did not
look upon then the shark fin hill, my father
pointing red kites in the grey no-one sees.
We close ourselves in fog, the dear
apparitions of day; most vague and indescribable light.
To exist here is ever to quiver, moraines of rainfall
in shift of melt, location service.
A coolness covers
the question of narrative; you speak
but it is so, it is not, it is every time.
I will not think of this as ending,
I draw the lines of familiar silence
where you fell, westerly
chopping the sky like a butternut
trying to get that seed,
sweetness; the flesh of a subject
in muscular chunks, just being.
Something needs ice and vitamins,
a violence outside
so we do not speak. It is noon
where you fell, and the air on my face.

ALICE
TARBUCK

The poem, in Alice Tarbuck's hands, is never mere diversion or entertainment, though nor can it be read without pleasure. Its affinity is with spells, prayers, talismans, which are not (or not merely) poetic forms, but ontological: forms for making being. Her poetry draws from the wellsprings of magic and ritual, revitalised in contemporary currents of feminist thought and the fraught and endangered networks of the everyday Anthropocene. Bold and subtle reimaginings of the (grid)lines between human and non-human, figure and ground, they are 'a space', as the closing lines of her 2018 pamphlet *Grid* (Sad Press) put it, 'small as a pin, to slip through / and perform our difference in'. This impetus is felt too in the present selection, a sequence which explores form through augury, and so makes the poems a kind of 'Action at a distance' both spatial and temporal. Such, as Tarbuck reminds us, 'is one of the possibilities of magic.'

Pip Augury

It's a filing system, pips arranged, radial nodes of DNA
moon-cresents — the casting is aghast with juice
the future is sticky, pings against
the metal sink. Secrets under the pith,
like gigglers getting gossip from the Priest —
the lambs entrails said *what?* — we always knew
Enochian angels, Adamical, pronunciate,
pouring out the mixer tap, proud of the queen.
     — a man once told me all life is vibration
          — played me guitar, gave me an amulet
          — full of desire. Augury fires against intention
          — like the first bursting plunk of a ripe sky

Sigh-matics: grasshopper orchestral painters, grass kaleidoscope
the nodal vibration modes all have central symmetry
so why
don't we all
    bounce?

Pips, pips, bone-white.
Fortune telling is classical
physics in the hands of men who are trying to sell you time.
Long loops, refraction, scrying, hope. The man on the moon
was got there by orange pips, held in a fine greaseproof packet
in case they would grow.
Bring crystal oscillators, jump the juice into intra-cellular patterns.
Everybody says it has nothing to do with growth, that you can't
mandala crops. But the pips say
play me Bach, bring me the best thing you sorry lot made
and I'll think about it.

Who supposes music isn't eaten, taken in
the same as sunlight.

Speak to the pips.
Bring them gifts. The future is just constellations waiting for the
        first eyes
to bump into them, waiting for the right dip
of the head or the plate or the portion of the pith.

Nephelomancy

Even the snow falls
against capital

Even the snow creeps late
to speak hot ground

Throwing the Bones

Action at a distance is one of the possibilities of magic.

Have you heard about red rain,
desert sand   heaved into the sky   and dropped
back
down.

Ideally the footnote is the solution to acidity,
hungry beyond reasonable
resource allocation. Just look at your wrist bones,
out in the more-than-human humidity of Charlottesville,
under the armed gaze whilst I'm trying to

talk
about
love

or wrists at least
but the text won't let that facism slip

like
a purl
stitch

like
a thrown
punch

like a sprained
wrist

One thing being as another is a form
of sideways magic, so look at where equivalence cracks,
crazy paves away into

THEY ARE THIS AND WE
ARE
THAT
AND WE HAVE GUNS THAT CONFIRM
EACH BIAS IN OUR FAVOUR, look

I could cry real actual tears and I bet I could get four
contiguous tears to hold inside the dip of your wristbone,
tasty shoal of grief   for you to

bolt
like an
oyster.

Enigmatic
aphrodisiac, that bone.
Look, it's about love, it's about licking my salt out of your dips,
it's about rows and rows of armed white men, faces strained against
difference, arms holding guns like guns,

a gun
does not have the right to comparative language,

me never actually rescuing you and being so glad, anyway,
that the plane took off. Insurance
covers
the bones.

Euhemerism

Tug the thread, see Ariadne fall
back into a spider, hear Boreas
whistle away down the gulley.

Even Socrates knows to mock
such small origination. Dark caves
hold on like mouths hold teeth —
open your fingers and see sparks,
you clever Prometheus, you clever
great big bang.

Ex Avibus

Oscines
The hospital car park is full of blackbirds, singing.

Alites
The courtroom sky-light is dark with birds in flight.

Runes

cannot prove a man hates women
unless he is against a wall or sitting a polygraph or has
a collection of their heads at home.

before the divinitive, conjecture.

have my hand in the bag before his hands
      look harm
And   about this is   beautiful
      the runes
                   .

      a priori sacred,
           until head is on table
wrong until
      head is on neck.

Not artificial but natural
after Coleridge

Ritual is pure activity without meaning or goal,
        without keening or shoal,
                kenning or

        All is ruinate,
        spires appease the human sense of viewmaking
        and everyone who comes leaves an apple at the stones
        instead.

Myths are not allegorical; rather tautegorical

instead of being one thing and signifying another,
they signify only what   they   are
this//is//my//body and the priest speaks and the god speaks
and the voice is
pure activity

stuff and appearance cannot be divided

is the cruciform hand in class, timer in kitchen, helpful pamphlet
    in waiting room
and the ritual is seek and use
the ritual is 'hello. who is speaking?'
knowing the answer (aleph, alec, how tall is Imhotep?)
sugar rim pilgrim crunch and open, lick and sing.

Boxes of crushed angels shaken out and held aloft
the cats ate the
tinsel and had to be made to be sick

Impetrative & Oblative

it comes, a rush
of wings
of blood-hot offal
of stains on the ground
when the ground
was supposed
to be clear

and the emperor faints

it comes by night
in the tip of ice
falling quietly into the sea
like Icarus,
the rev of a motor
over the banked height
of trees

and the emperor feints

it comes with such ease,
the end — like a swallow,
a dry kiss on the edge of a cheek
like a beak tapping against a door
waiting to be let fly
waiting to tell its meaning out by
accident

and the emperor lifts
his small white hand and asks
to see the trick again.

KATE TOUGH

Kate Tough is a found poet *par excellence*, her craft one of discovery, superimposition and recontextualisation. While the means are often deceptively slight, the ends are strange, complex, forceful, at once charming and unsettling, funny and disturbing, as Tough's overhearings are underwritten with sharp political and social critique. Her 2016 pamphlet *tilt-shift* (Tapsalteerie), runner-up in the 2017 Callum Macdonald Memorial Award, reveals an astonishing propensity for finding poetry in the most unlikely places, confirming – contra Auden – that poetry is making everything happen, all of the time. The pamphlet also features the caustic 'People Made Glasgow', selected as a Best Scottish Poem 2016, which lays bare the 'Shame in our hulls' of Scotland's colonial past. The present selection segues from the concerns of *tilt-shift* to, among other things, our present malaise, with Tough's work making for an urgent and necessary 'barbed' response to the politics of hatred and division.

Caitlin

Okay, the plan is
to make a secret book
(at afterschool) and
write fake secrets
about people
we don't like.
Then we go to play
and "accidentally"
leave the book
then Tess will read it
and blab it
to everyone.

Contents found on a piece of folded paper
on a primary school floor. Names changed.

Barbed

Designed to pen livestock
its potential wasn't lost on the military.

This video has no sound.
Hundreds strung. Hung in grotesque

postures as though praying;
died on their knees and the wire

prevented their fall. Often
couldn't see the wire until under fire.

Letter to Girlfriend.
It is simply murder.

-

93-year-old Ruby Barber was raided
for the fourth time. A thief climbed
over the fence and sneaked into
the frail widow's bungalow.

Mrs Barber, who made boots for soldiers during the Second
World War, has vowed to fight on. Her son Burt spent £450
erecting barbed wire around her

garden fence and roof.
"I didn't put the wire up because
I liked putting it up. But life is not ideal.
The Queen has got barbed wire

around Buckingham Palace. Well
with all due respect, my mother is my
queen to me." Mrs Barber hasn't been
a victim in the 18 months since.

-

The razor wire can be winded around the garden fence
to add extra security and safety, and the design of blades
keeps unwanted guests out of your garden and
avoids mischievous intrusion.

The razor wire can be winded around the perimeter fence
and the design of blades keeps unwanted men/women/children
of a different nationality/religion/colour/income bracket out of
your country/occupied territory/more valuable or fertile area and
avoids mischievous attempts to access resources.

The razor wire can be winded around the detention centre fence
and the design of blades keeps unwanted guests
inside your facility and
avoids mischievous attempts to obtain asylum/a fair trial/freedom.

-

Q: Is razor wire suitable for segregating cattle?
   The answer is emphatically no!

-

BUY IN THE SHOP

Heavy Duty High Tensile Galvanised

For use when economy is the priority.

NATO Razor Wire Accessory Set

Ideal for protecting your hands and wrists from cuts and puncture wounds whilst forming barbed wire coils.

Freely Rotating Anti-scaling Anti-climb

Designed to effectively roll away aggression and crime.

Rusty Barbed Wire Garland

12ft (string) garland in rusty barbed wire design.
Great for decorating at any western themed party.

Text found 3rd Jan 2018 at: http://online.wsj.com/ww1/barbed-wire ; https://spartacus-educational.com/FWWbarbed.htm (incl. George Coppard & Jack Sweeney) ; http://www.dailymail.co.uk/news/article-65450/Anger-barbed-wire-row.html ; razorwireuk.com ; manomano.co.uk ; vandgard.co.uk ; partypacks.co.uk

(E)VOLVE(R)

MORE TRUE STORIES OF PEOPLE WHO HAVE HAD
CONTACT WITH BREXITEERS & HOW *YOU* CAN TOO!

1.

I'm often asked, "How do I know the difference between true
angelic communication and the Brexit campaign?"

There are several characteristics to notice:

True Angelic Guidance	*The Brexit Campaign*
Loving and warm	Negative and abusive
Supportive	Discouraging
Brief and to the point	Overly verbal
Talks about how you can help others	Talks about how you can get something from others
Encourages you to pursue your dreams	Doubts whether your dreams can come true
Inspires you to develop your talents	Distracts you from applying your talents
Asks you to balance your time usage	Guides you to over-focus on one life area

2.

You can request help from Farage, Johnson, Rees-Mogg (or other hardline Brexiteers), members of the European Research Group, or local activists in so many ways:

- Think the thought, "Help me!"

- Invite them into your dreams

- Ask for a sign

You are surrounded by Brexiteers right now. Even if you're a non-believer, you have Leave supporters who love you, and who are with you, at this very moment. Close your eyes, breathe deeply, and feel their presence. If you still can't sense the will of the people, keep going. The Brexit fanatics are even more motivated to make their presence known than you are. They care so much and want to become more involved in your life.

3.

Most people have had a Brexit-means-Brexit experience. Gut or intuitive feelings are probably the most common example. But there are also more profound ways to experience EU exit crusaders, including the following:

Brushing against you. Feeling someone or something touch, or move across, your skin or hair. It's not as creepy as it sounds.

Sensing a particular person's presence. When you sense that an architect of extreme Brexit is with you, chances are that you're correct. Each person has a unique energy "fingerprint", and we can sense which self-serving Leave champion entered the room.

Feeling your ear pinched. Very often, our Brexit guides pull our earlobes as a way of goading us along. If this sensation is ever painful, please tell your guide to find a gentler way to lead you on the path.

Someone tucking you in. You're having a difficult time sleeping, but then you feel a presence beside you. You know that it's Nigel Farage. The next thing you know, you have blankets pulled over you, and you're tucked in.

Stomach or jaw sensations. You enter a roomful of people and your stomach tightens. The body acts like a divining instrument that ferrets out whether something or someone is trying to take back control.

Sudden pain or illness. You feel fine, your health is good, and you have been treating your body with care. But then you have an attack of pain or illness from out of nowhere. It feels like you have been ambushed. Well, chances are that you have been. When people with big red buses and sophisticated social media algorithms are manipulating you, studies show that your heart rate and blood pressure increase.

Sensing that something's off, or just not right. Someone invites you to participate in a deal … but something feels off about the deal. You decide against participating, and a year later, you read that those who did participate are suing for fraud.

Psychic lovemaking. You're a female in bed and you feel the energy of a male Leave campaigner hovering near you. You realise the ardent Leaver is making gestures of foreplay. Please be careful when allowing a hard Brexiteer to engage sexually with you. Insist they go away. If you've made love to such a person in the past, just put it behind you, and make a vow to only share your body with lovers of the highest spiritual caliber from now on.

Brexit Visions II: Text found in Doreen Virtue's Angel Visions II: More True Stories of People Who Have Had Contact With Angels, And How You Can, Too! (Hay House, 2006).

Over page, *Islip*: Station names found on the Long Island Rail Road, 30 May, 2016.

About the editor

Calum Rodger is a poet and critic based in Glasgow. He has published and presented research on the Makars, digital poetics, and 'avant-gardener' Ian Hamilton Finlay, among other topics, while his published pamphlets include *Know Yr Stuff: Poems on Hedonism* (Tapsalteerie, 2014) and *PORTS* (SPAM, 2019). He has written for publications such as *Glasgow Review of Books* and *The Island Review*, ran live poetry night The Verse Hearse with Stewart Sanderson from 2012 to 2016, and is Scottish National Slam Champion 2019. Professional roles include Co-Director of the Scottish Universities' International Summer School, Prisons Co-Ordinator with Open Book, Poetry & Poetics tutor at the University of Glasgow, and Poetry Reviews Editor at *Gutter Magazine*. His latest pamphlet *Rock, Star, North.* – a poetic travelogue set in the Grand Theft Auto universe – is forthcoming from Tapsalteerie.